Robert Baden

TEEN TALKS WITH GOD

Publishing House
St. Louis

Cover photos by Wallowitch; photo p. 65 by Mimi Forsyth; all other photos by Wallowitch

This book may not be reproduced in whole or in part, by mimeograph or any other means, without permission. For information, address: Concordia Publishing House, 3558 S. Jefferson Ave., St. Louis, MO 63118.

All rights reserved
Copyright © 1980 Concordia Publishing House
Printed in the United States of America

Library of Congress Cataloging in Publication Data

Baden, Robert, 1936—
   Teen talks with God.

     1. Youth—Religious life. I. Title.
BV4531.2.B23   248.8′3   80-323
ISBN 0-570-03812-X

For our past, present, and
future teenagers:
Brent, Brenda,
Daniel, and Corwin

Contents

Automobiles	9
Brothers and Sisters	10
Companions	12
Dating	15
Education	17
Fathers and Mothers	18
God	20
Health and Appearance	25
Intelligence	27
Jealousy	29
Kicks	32
Love	34
Money	37
Narcotics	40
Occupations	42
Prejudice	47
Questions	48
Religion	53
Sex	55
Tensions	58
Unbelief	61
Vulgarity	64
Wisdom	66
(X) Pornography	70
Youth	73
(Z) Death	77

A Word from the Author

No one has to tell you that the teen years are a turbulent time of your life. It's hard to predict just how you will be feeling tomorrow, much less next week. You are sitting on a seesaw: One minute you're up, the next minute you're down.

Well, this is nothing new for teenagers, but it is for you. And as the father of teenagers, and remembering my own teen years, I think I understand what you are going through. In these pages I've tried to go through the alphabet of teen experiences and show how you might want to talk them over with that Friend who will never let you down: God, your Creator and loving Redeemer.

If you are tongue-tied when it comes to putting your thoughts and feelings into words, maybe these prayer thoughts can get you started. Once you get going, just let loose and say what's on *your* mind and in your heart. And since I'm sure I missed some of your personal concerns—why don't you add to this alphabetical list and write out your own prayer thoughts. Either way or both, you can be sure of one thing: God, your Father in heaven, is listening at the other end of the line. And He cares.

Automobiles

I like cars, God, just about anything with wheels and a motor—cars, trucks, motorcycles. I like to think of myself driving clear across the world, sitting there behind the wheel of a shined-up, well-cared-for car. I've saved, I've shopped, I've rebuilt, I've polished—and now it's mine.

Or even if it's only the folks' car. I love to drive. I love to have my friends see me drive. It makes me feel good inside, all over; it makes me feel special.

Oh, God, I know I misuse the privilege I have to drive. I like to drive fast, faster than the speed limit, for sure, especially when someone's with me. Is that showing off? Or just enjoying speed? I like speed. I like the windows open and wind and going fast. Is it wrong to want to know how fast my car'll go?

I like to take off quickly from a stop sign; it feels good to hear the squeal of the tires. It's like a challenge, a dare to do it better than anyone else. And to tell the truth, I like it even when down deep I know it's wrong, wasteful, even stupid.

Sometimes it scares me. I've taken chances that I shouldn't have, whipped around a corner or into traffic when I shouldn't have. I know it's dangerous to take chances like that, for me and for others with me, for those in other cars or walking. How can I keep from doing it when I like it?

Ride with me, God. Let me remember that You're right beside me, not just to warn me or scare me into obeying the law, but to protect me and to help me say no to myself or to others who dare me to speed or drive recklessly.

Not everyone has a car. Not everyone even gets to drive like I do. Thanks, God, for letting me have the chance. Thanks for being with me and for taking care of me. Don't leave me—ever—even when I act like I want nothing to do with You. I'll probably be driving the rest of my life, and I'll need You when I'm an adult too. Let me start getting used to having You as my regular passenger.

Thanks for listening. It helps—a lot. I feel better already.

Brothers and Sisters

Sometimes, God, my brothers or sisters almost drive me out of my mind! Older ones make fun of me or act so superior. I have to wear their old clothes, and my parents always compare me to them—and you don't have to be all-knowing to guess who comes out second best!

Younger brothers or sisters always want to be with me or go with me wherever I go. There are times now, God, that I'd rather be alone. I need to be alone to think or to talk to You like this. They get on my nerves, God. And I really feel guilty when I find myself thinking that I really don't like my own brothers and sisters.

I don't want to feel this way. I want to love them and enjoy being with them. I don't want to yell at them for messing with my things; I want to be able to learn from older brothers and sisters and to teach the younger ones,

so they have it a little less rough than I do. I guess I need You again, God, like always.

Down deep I *am* proud of my brothers and sisters. I like to watch the older ones and to know that we're related. And younger brothers and sisters are so cute, so innocent. I like to peek into their rooms when they're sleeping—they really do look like angels then.

It's not easy to have brothers and sisters. I know what I ought to do and what I ought to feel. I'm sure the older ones are frustrated by their problems and don't need me to bother them with mine. And the younger ones are frustrated because they're always being told they have to wait until they're older to do what I get to do. They need me, though, to help and to listen. And even the older ones need my support; they need me to show how proud I really am of them.

Let me do that, God. Let me take that extra step to help my brothers and sisters, older or younger, in any way I can. Sure, I have problems, but maybe if I think a bit more about their problems and look for ways to help them, my own won't seem so big. Maybe they'll even take the time to help me with mine. Thanks, God.

Companions

Why is it, God, that when I don't have all the friends I'd like to have, I feel bad; and when I do have friends, I feel bad because they don't always come through the way I wish they would? How can I make those people I'd like to have as my friends become aware that I even exist? And how can I convince my parents that I *can* make wise choices of friends?

I guess I'm pretty full of questions today, God. Thanks for not minding and thanks for always helping me find the answers I need. So many of the problems and frustrations in my life come as a result of my friends—or lack of friends.

I want to be liked. Everyone does. And I want to be liked by people who are liked by everyone, the popular kids. I try to be friendly, I try to do the things they do, I try to get their attention without being obnoxious, but they don't seem to notice. Am I doing something wrong? What *should* I do?

I like being with my friends, but I don't always agree with what they say or do. I don't know whether to speak up or walk away or what. I don't want to lose their friendship, but I don't always like their actions. What do I do then, God?

And my folks are so suspicious of my friends; they seem to assume the worst if my friends' clothing styles or hair styles or language or even the kind of cars they drive are different from their own. They don't seem to realize that friendship isn't based on superficial things. What do I do?

Oh, sure, I make mistakes about friends sometimes, but I can correct them too. People in the Bible had friends that didn't turn out the way they'd hoped they would; even Judas didn't turn out to be what Jesus had wanted.

I think I know the kind of friends I ought to have. But I also need You—and I guess my parents too—to remind me. And I know, too, that You are watching me and will direct me and others toward friendships with each other. Keep an eye on me, God; I may not always sound like I really want You to see me, but I really don't want to make mistakes.

And thanks for listening. It really helps a lot just to talk it out with You.

Dating

Every time I think about dating, God, I start feeling uncomfortable or mixed up inside. I'm not sure exactly why. I want to date, I think; at least it seems like everyone else is either dating or talking about it. But I'm still uneasy.

It's so tough for a guy to pick up a phone and call a girl he doesn't really know, and it's so tough for a girl to wait for that call. Even in these changing times when a girl is supposed to be able to take the initiative it's still uncomfortable.

And being on a date isn't easy, either. It seems like I can't think of things to say; we just sit there, both feeling uneasy. And there's so much pressure to play a kind of game. I mean, should I try to hold her hand? Or let him hold my hand? Or initiate or allow a kiss? There's so much pressure to do the "right thing" that it's hard to just enjoy being with someone that I want to be with. Starting to date isn't easy, God!

And how do you avoid getting too serious too soon? Sure, going steady takes off the pressure of finding a date for some event, but I'm not ready to get that serious. And going steady increases the pressure, the temptations to go too far, to initiate or allow things that I'm not comfortable with or that are wrong and are just another chapter in "doing the expected thing."

Give me strength, God, as I enter and go through the dating phase of my life. I know dating helps prepare me for marriage and spending my life with someone special of the other sex. Give me confidence and give me wisdom. I know I'm growing up and becoming an adult; I feel it and I see it. It's good to know and feel that I'm normal and attractive to someone else, and it's good to know I can talk to You about how I feel. Stay with me, God. Direct me toward the kinds of people that You approve of, ones that will treat me with the respect that I want to give them.

Thanks, God, You always understand so well, even when my words are a little hard in coming.

Education

God, school gets me down some days. When I look at the stack of books I have to read and the list of papers I have to write, I wonder if it's all worthwhile. Oh, sure, I want to finish high school, and I know I ought to go on to college or some other kind of school, but I'm tired of so much of the stuff we have to do. I really can't see the reason for it, although my folks keep saying it's all important. I know I'm not sure yet what my career will be, but I *know* some of this is ridiculous!

Even when I want to study, the extracurricular stuff keeps popping up. I'm expected to go to games, plays, meetings—all that kind of thing—and something's got to give. I'm just scared it might be me. Do I risk flunking a test in order to attend something else I'm supposed to?

It helps to talk to You about it, God, even when I'm busy and ought to read the next chapter in English. When I talk to You, I can hear You talking back to me. You keep saying things like, "I'll give you the strength you need." Or, "Just hang in there; I'll take care of you." And that helps, even when I have a little trouble really believing You will. The year is passing so quickly and so will each one until I'm out of high school—and college, maybe. I don't know where the time goes. I just know I'm tired. But You understand. You know how busy I am. Even Jesus got tired and needed to rest, like the time all those people wanted Him to heal them or just wanted a piece of His time. He went away to talk to You about it too. And when He did, He always came back stronger and more ready to do what He had to do.

God, I know You understand, and I know You love me. Help me now when I'm in this bind. Give me that extra boost to make it through this week—and the one after that. You sent angels to give Jesus strength. That's all I need, just to know You're near, just to know You care, even when others don't seem to. Thanks, God, for listening. I think I can finish that chapter now—and the math assignment, too. I'll make it—with You.

Fathers and Mothers

Thank You, God, for fathers and mothers. Even though there are lots of times that they say things that I can't understand, I love them. Help me find ways to show them how I feel.

I do wish they would understand me better, though. I know they're concerned about me all the time, but they really seem not to trust me. Oh, sure, I've done enough things that were stupid or wrong to give them plenty reasons to wonder if I'll ever be trustworthy, but I am learning all the time, even by those mistakes.

Parents worry about a lot of things—money, education, me, each other, health, their parents—things like that. And they argue about those things sometimes, even fight about them. I don't know if they know that I notice, but I do; and sometimes I wish I didn't. It makes me wonder sometimes if I want to grow up and get married and raise children.

Are they right when they say things about my friends? And can't they believe me when I tell them I am selective? Why do they assume that I'm doing something wrong when I'm with my friends, or when I stay out later

than they think I should? I want to please my parents, but I can't be like them in every way or live my life the way they do. I don't think I'd even want to be exactly like them. I am me, after all!

I would like to be able to talk comfortably with them, though—together and one at a time—without winding up in an argument. They do have a lot of experience with life, and they know a lot more than I do about many things that I'm worried about. But they seem uncomfortable talking about those things, although sometimes I probably make it awfully hard for them to discuss things with me. But I do need them, and I do appreciate all they try to do, even when they try too hard or when I make it difficult for them.

Let me show them I love them and need them, God. Give me patience to control my temper when they make me mad. Help me reach out to them and make them feel comfortable with me. I'm sure it's not easy being a parent, and I know it's not easy being a teenager. Show us how much we need each other, God. And thanks!

God

How can I talk to You about You, God? It feels kind of silly, but I certainly don't know everything about You that I'd like to know or that I should know. It's easy to talk to You about other things, but this feels strange. Bear with me if I seem awkward and have trouble finding the right words. I don't want to ask the wrong things, but I know You'll understand.

You must feel disappointed that so many people act like or say that You don't exist. After all You've done,

too! When I hear them treat You like the imagination of primitive people, I get angry, partly because of what they say and partly because I don't do a very good job of telling others about You. If I'm too direct, they either laugh at me or ignore me; so usually I just try to show that I know You indirectly, by wearing a cross or going to church or talking about You as if there were no question about Your reality.

It bothers me a lot when people use Your name in profanity. They usually use it without thinking or to show how "mature" they are, I think. I try not to do that myself, but maybe I should do something to discourage others. Speaking up doesn't seem to work at all, though, so I usually just excuse myself from a group that is heading that direction. But is that best? Is that what You want me to do?

And sometimes You don't seem as real or as close as You are at other times, even to me. Now and then I even ask myself if You are really beside me, hearing everything I say or think. I do have doubts sometimes about Your hand being in all things or that You really see all we do or all that happens in the world. Sometimes I ask why You allow some things to happen.

I'm sorry for these doubts. I know better. You've given me a world and family and a life full of the evidence of Your love. And You've given me the Bible and Your words of promise. You even gave Your own Son for me, and You give me the faith to accept Him as my Savior. Yes, I know You and I love You, God!

I'm not asking You for visible reminders. Just work inside me and give me strength. I know that the moment I believe You don't exist would be the moment I'd be without hope. I feel Your hand in mine, God. Thanks for being You.

Health and Appearance

Every time I look in the mirror, God, I find something I don't like. Right now I just can't get my hair to look right, and I'm having trouble covering a new blemish. Why is it so hard to be satisfied with the looks You've given me, God? I'd change so many things if I could.

And I'm tired all the time. Mom thinks I must have "mono," and dad says I don't eat right or get enough sleep. I *do* take vitamins, and I certainly get enough exercise. I know I'm growing and changing a lot right now, and I know that takes a lot of energy. But why does it have to be so hard to be a teenager?

I know I'm complaining, and I'm sorry, God. You have given me so much, and I should be grateful even if I don't have the looks of a movie star or the health and stamina of an Olympic athlete. But my friends are so conscious of looks and actions and all those things that aren't nearly as important as just being myself. How can I handle this pressure to look a certain way or to act a certain way in order to have friends and get a little attention? Am I too vain? Should I just be a slob and forget whether my hair is styled right or whether my clothes are okay, not too old and not too new?

I know You don't want that, God. After all, whatever I have, whatever I am, whatever way I look or feel, is part of me and one of Your gifts. My body is the greatest of Your creations, and I know You expect me to keep it running right. Maybe that means eating a balanced meal

when I'd rather have a hamburger and a shake. And I believe it means taking care of my hair and skin and teeth and everything else that is part of me as best I can, even when the final product won't make the cover of a fashion magazine.

Most important, You've given me a mind and common sense. Help me use them to understand and do what I can to stay healthy and to package the product I have as well as I can. Help me remember that I reflect You—whatever I do and however I look. I am the only "me" I've got; help me to like "me" just the way I am, just the way You wanted me to be.

Thanks, God, for what I am and what I can be through You!

Intelligence

God, we had our annual IQ tests the other day, and I have my annual case of nerves about it. And judging by the things the other kids are saying, I wasn't the only one concerned. Teachers and parents make such a big deal about IQs and whether it means I'm hopeless or a genius or college potential or whatever. It just gets a bit scary when someone suggests that my whole future might depend on what this test shows.

I mean, what can I *do* about it? I'm *me*, both before and after I take this test. If I score 80, does that mean I'm nothing? If my score is 150, is my future guaranteed? Of course not! What really gets me is that no one tells me what I scored, just things like, "Your IQ test shows that you're not working up to your potential." Does anyone? Ever? Does that mean those who are doing just as well as they ought to—no better, no worse—are the best people in the world?

I know I'm no genius, but I'm sure not a nothing either. I can do some things well and other things not so well. Sometimes I goof off, but sometimes I do better than I thought I could. But I'm probably not ever just exactly what some test says I am or should be.

I know IQ tests are helpful in determining potential ability, but I also know such tests aren't always accurate because of backgrounds and cultures and things like that. I just wish people would stop comparing me to my friends or brothers and sisters; they either make me feel like I'm falling short of my potential or overachieving.

At least You understand. I know You're in control of these things. Whatever I have comes from You, and if You gave it, it must be good and right and enough. I know You want me to use it as well as I can, to keep reaching and to keep trying. You also understand failing and facing reality. Give me strength to work and reach and succeed, and give me a boost when I fail or simply can't do something. And thanks for hearing me, God, and treating me like "me" when everyone else can see only numbers and potential and comparisons with others.

Jealousy

Why is it so often that others get what I'm seeking? They win when I lose. They get the good breaks. Are they any better or smarter or more talented than I am? Maybe they have inside information or get some special treatment from others. I don't know what it is, God, but I'm fed up and frustrated and ready to quit. Isn't it my turn to be

Number One?

Wow, God, listen to me! Even though I know that You always know what I'm thinking, it's still hard to say out loud to You what I'm thinking. I hope being jealous is part of being a teenager, but whether it is or not, I'm jealous right now. I know it's wrong, and maybe that's why I have to tell You about it. I think I need Your help with the "Green-Eyed Monster" that's eating inside me.

I know my talents. I really try to get involved in things, to use what I have to the best of my ability. Sure, I like the credit too, but that's not the only reason. You say that I'm supposed to *use* my talents, not hide them, but then someone else makes the team, gets the part, or is selected for choir or band or elected to some class office. And I get nothing! That's why I'm jealous; I don't even get to use my talents when I try to use them. It just isn't fair that someone else is always the winner.

Well, maybe not always, God. I can't lie to You. I may not have gotten the part I wanted or gotten to start the game or been selected to first chair because there was someone who was more qualified. I guess it *is* mostly my ego. I do hope You understand when I want to be the hero. So do the others, and they really have talents too. I wish I could be more sincere when I congratulate them, though, and not feel so bitter, so jealous inside. I'm sorry, God.

Help me, God. Let me be a good sport, one who can rejoice even when someone else scores the important goal. Help me to keep my confidence and to keep on trying. I've got to believe that You have something planned for me, some role for which I'm suited. Make me to see it when it comes, and help me accept it. And until then, give me strength to always do my best. I know now this wasn't yet the time for me. But thanks to You, God, I know it's coming!

Kicks

I guess You know how many times kids my age talk about doing something for "kicks," God. You probably get pretty tired of hearing that as a reason or an excuse for the kinds of things teenagers do. I get tired of it too, but for a different reason, I'm sure.

I like to do fun things, God, but so many times they border on things I know are wrong. And the older I get, the harder it is to say no. It's like the kids just expect everyone to go along with whoever can come up with the wildest idea. And it's no secret to You that I don't always say no, even when I know better. I'm sorry, but it's so hard to handle all these temptations; I really need Your help.

I want to keep my friends. I want to be part of the group. I want to have fun. But I don't want this constant pull between the right and wrong or almost wrong. So I guess a lot of times I go along to a party, go along on a ride, go along with a group to a show or to get something to eat and tell myself that I'm not going to cross the line I've set for myself. Sometimes it works. But it feels uncomfortable, and too often I bend the line more than I'd like. I feel like I should stand up and try to stop the excesses of others, but that just doesn't work. How can I be part of the group and not part of it at the same time? How can I handle this mad dash for "kicks"?

I know You're listening, and I know You want to help, God. I know You've said things about letting my light shine. Maybe others are also looking for a way to

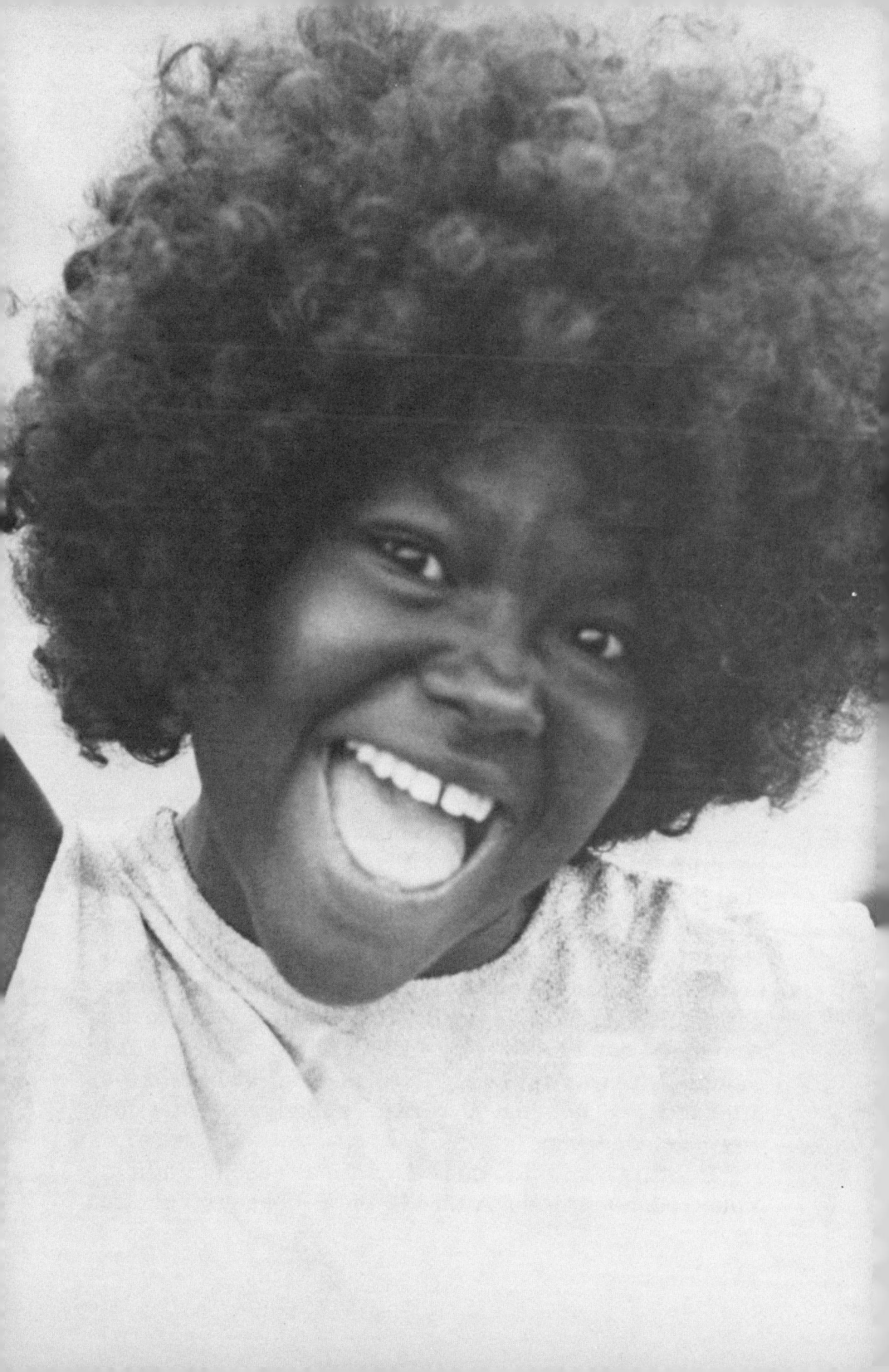

say no. Maybe they feel caught up in the pressure too. Maybe most of the others *would* respect me if I said no when it started getting out of hand. Sure, I may get laughed at or called a few names, but I think I can show I like or admire people for reasons other than their ability to get "kicks." It sure won't be easy, but I think I can live easier getting called names than doing things I know are wrong. God, at those times when I need help, remind me of Jesus and how He refused to bend to pressure. Remind me how He said no to Satan, even when the Tempter offered Him the kingdoms of the world. Give me the strength to stand firm at the line that You've helped me draw, God. Let me share the light I have because of You. Help me commit my life more to You, and let Your service be my biggest "kick" of all.

Love

You know, God, I think "love" is just maybe the most poorly used word in the English language. I've been keeping track, and in the past week I've heard Sue say she "loves" hamburgers, Jon "loves" football, Jason "loves" to swim, Marsha "loves" Brian, and Brian "loves" his English teacher. Two guys on the basketball team were talking about "loving" the new offense they're using this year, and Anne just "loves" an eastern accent. And me? I don't know what I think or what I love, but I thought love was a special kind of feeling you had for the opposite sex, not just a word to show preference for anything, anytime.

But this confusion does give me a reason to talk to You, God, about love. After all, the Bible says You *are*

Love, and that ought to make You the expert I need. I'm growing up, I know, and I think more and more about love and that special person I'll meet someday and share the rest of my life with. I see someone attractive and ask myself, "Could that be the one?" "Could I love that person enough to share everything with him (or her)?" Oh, sure, I've liked people I've dated or danced with. Once or twice I even thought I might love one of them, but I don't know now. I may not be quite ready yet—at least I know my parents don't think so—but I sure am getting closer, God.

  I don't know if bells will ring or if I'll feel warm and weak all over, but I hope it will be special, certainly not like hamburgers or swimming or a new car. And when that time comes, when I "fall in love," be with me, God. Make me look with my mind when You see me looking only with my eyes and heart. Make that person someone I like to see and someone that I respect and who respects me. Make it more than a physical attraction; make it a love that comes from inside. Let it be someone a lot like me and one who has talents and strengths I lack. If possible, make it someone who also loves You and who can talk to You with me. I know it's probably a good while off yet, God, but thanks for not laughing when I talk about it. And thanks for helping me get ready.

Money

  I'm broke again, God. I just don't know where my money goes. It seems like so much when I get paid or when I get a gift or an allowance, but by the time the weekend or something special comes along, it's just not there. Sure, I could work more or get a different job, but that cuts into school and everything else. My folks want me to take part in school activities and be able to go out with my friends, but if I work more, I couldn't do that and get my homework done too. But it would sure be nice to have another $10 now and then—or even a dollar or two a week more.

I tried to budget several times. You know, so much for snacks or pizza, so much for other things I want or need, something for clothes, something for going out with friends, even something for church, but it never seems to work out. There's always a bill I didn't expect or something I need for school or want very badly.

The scary thing is that I hear mom and dad worrying exactly the same way. They talk about how much things used to cost and what they cost now. They're trying to save up to help me through college, but they have all kinds of bills they didn't expect either, for utilities or medical care or gasoline. I *can't* ask them for any more, although they do try to help out. I know it isn't right to worry all the time about money—but I do.

God, show me some way around this problem. Should I change jobs? Should I quit something at school so I can work? Or quit school? I know You're probably not going to lay the answer right out on my desk for me, but I do hear You saying that You will provide for me. I do see the flowers and the birds and see Your care for them; I know You'll take care of me. And that helps. Maybe if I'd stop worrying quite so much I'd be better able to consider my options.

Thanks, God, I feel better already. Sure, I may not get any more money out of this, but at least I can stop worrying so much about it. You're real, You're here with me, and I know it! And I believe that it will work out— You *will* show me an answer in Your own way and time.

I'm certainly ready whenever You are—and I know You're always ready for me. Thanks, God.

Narcotics

I'm going to let "narcotics" include some other things, God, tobacco and alcohol to be specific. Drugs and smoking and drinking seem to be part of the same problem, all those things that are so ready to make life miserable for me. And it's a problem that's no longer unusual. I know these things are common in high school, and I guess junior highs and even grade schools have problems with these things.

It's easy to tell myself that only drugs are bad, that smoking—even marijuana—and drinking are somehow not so serious. But they can be, for teenagers and adults alike. I guess anything that can do to my body what drugs and drinking and tobacco can do is bad—period.

But it's hard to convince anyone—even myself—that this is true when I know how easy it is to get them. Anyone can get cigarettes, and it doesn't take a lot to get around the age law and get beer or wine or something stronger. Even drugs, in spite of stronger laws, are there if anyone wants them. Even those adults who really do seem concerned can't do anything about them. And judging by the stories I hear and the evidence I see and smell, it's getting worse, God.

I don't think anyone would touch these things if it were just the things themselves that were involved. But the image of being grown up if you smoke cigarettes or pot, if you drink and can hold your liquor, and if you've tried harder drugs is an awfully big part of the tempta-

tion. We all want to be grown up—or thought of as being grown up—and it's easy to get the idea that this is the quickest way to get there, at least in the eyes of my peers. And God, You know the pressures and tensions people have: grades, popularity, family problems, sports. All these things do their part to tempt someone who wants to tune out on the troubles they're having.

And, God, these things just don't tempt others; I feel it too. Sure, I can say no. But not without Your help. I want to be mature and popular. I get just as frustrated with school and parents and friends as anyone else. It's real, all the time. I know what You want me to do, but I need to be reminded. I need Your strength to turn my back, to walk away, to speak up, but I know it won't be easy, God. Somewhere I'll fall, I'm sure, but I know You'll pick me up and understand. More important, You'll help me stand up the next time. Please help me, God; these things have me really scared. Don't let me forget You're always there to say, "Don't be afraid, I'm with you."

Occupations

What am I going to be? What am I going to do with my life? Here I am in high school and I don't have the slightest idea which direction I should go. I don't know if I should go to college or start working as soon as I can to earn money. I want to *like* what I do, God, but right now I can't imagine doing anything 40 hours a week, 50 weeks a year, year after year after year. How do I plan for what will probably be the biggest part of my life? Can you help, God?

Sure, they've given me tests to see how smart I am and how well I'm doing, tests to see what interests I have and tests to direct me toward certain kinds of classes. But tests don't tell it all. I have to feel that whatever I do is meaningful and worthwhile, more than just a way to make more money than some other way, more than just a way to spend time and stay out of trouble. And I want to feel a sense of success, God, to have a chance for advancement and the chance to influence and perhaps lead others. How do I get ready for that, God?

It's not that I'm afraid of work. I've had part-time jobs—paper route, baby-sitting, yard work—but that's different. And people have commented on my talents; some have said I'd make a good computer programmer or teacher or lawyer, but is that what I want? Shouldn't I see clearly by now.?

I feel that You're near me, God. I feel You are standing here with an arm around me. I think I hear You saying, "Wait a bit; give yourself a chance to learn and try and think a bit more." Is that Your voice, God, or my imagination? It's hard to wait and not worry. I see my parents' money problems and job frustrations. I see people changing jobs and moving again and again, even when they're middle-aged or older. That doesn't make occupational life look too secure or satisfying to me! Are You sure, God, that I shouldn't jump in at once and get what I can? Are You really there, God?

I know You are. You always have been, and You're not going to skip out on me just when I need Your guidance so badly. I will trust You; I have to. I will wait and look and plan. I will talk to others and try to imagine how certain jobs might feel. I will try honestly to consider my skills and talents. And I'll remember that whatever I find, I'll do it with my whole might, knowing You are my Partner and my Friend. Open my eyes, God;

let me see Your way for me. Make me a tool in Your hands, and let me serve You whatever I do. Thanks for the advice, God; You understand so well what I need.

Prejudice

I used to think that the only prejudice was racial, God, like whites and blacks and things like that. Well, I know You're well aware of it, but every day I'm seeing prejudice more and more in other areas too. We really have a problem accepting each other as we are. It must be bad when people talk about "tolerance" as the ultimate goal as if putting up with someone you don't like is a real accomplishment. Almost no one talks about *loving* people who are different—except You, that is.

I know my friends and I reflect the prejudices we learned at home or in grade school, but here in high school it's awfully evident. Rich kids look down on poor kids—and vice versa; farm kids ridicule kids from the suburbs or the inner city. Attractive people exclude from their groups those who are less attractive; "party kids" criticize those who have other interests. Athletes snub musicians. Even kids that study and work for good grades are looked down on by those who see high school as a time to barely get by. Oh, sure, God, kids from any one of the races—black, white, red, yellow—are suspicious of anyone else and make it rough on those who try to erase the color barriers. Even the church does a poor job much of the time—pitting one kind of Methodist or Lutheran against another kind of Methodist or Lutheran, pitting one denomination against all other Protestants, against Roman Catholics, against Jewish people, or even against those who aren't in any church. Don't they hear Your Word, God, when You say that *all* of us are Your children, that You love everyone and want all of us to be saved and go to heaven? Doesn't even the church hear You, God?

We know so little about each other, and we don't seem to care enough to learn more. We seem to enjoy being able to look down on someone else, to keep in place those we fear or don't understand. We'd rather ridicule other languages than learn to speak them, tell ethnic jokes rather than appreciate another culture's food and clothing and customs. Your world is so varied and so interesting! Please, God, teach us to enjoy it and grow from experiences in it.

I make it sound like I'm perfect and have no prejudices. You know better! Give me strength to reach out and open doors, not close them. Help me take the risk to become acquainted with those who are different. Help me put aside my prejudice and start to learn what others are really like. We are all Your children. Help me, God.

Questions

Do You remember, God, how my parents used to shake their heads and say to me almost in desperation, "You ask so many questions! Give us a little rest"? They don't say it any more, God, not because I don't have any more questions, but because I've stopped asking them out loud. But You know I still have them. Maybe You're shaking Your head too, God, with all those questions I've been asking during our talks. But I know You really don't mind, and so I'll probably keep asking them. I'm

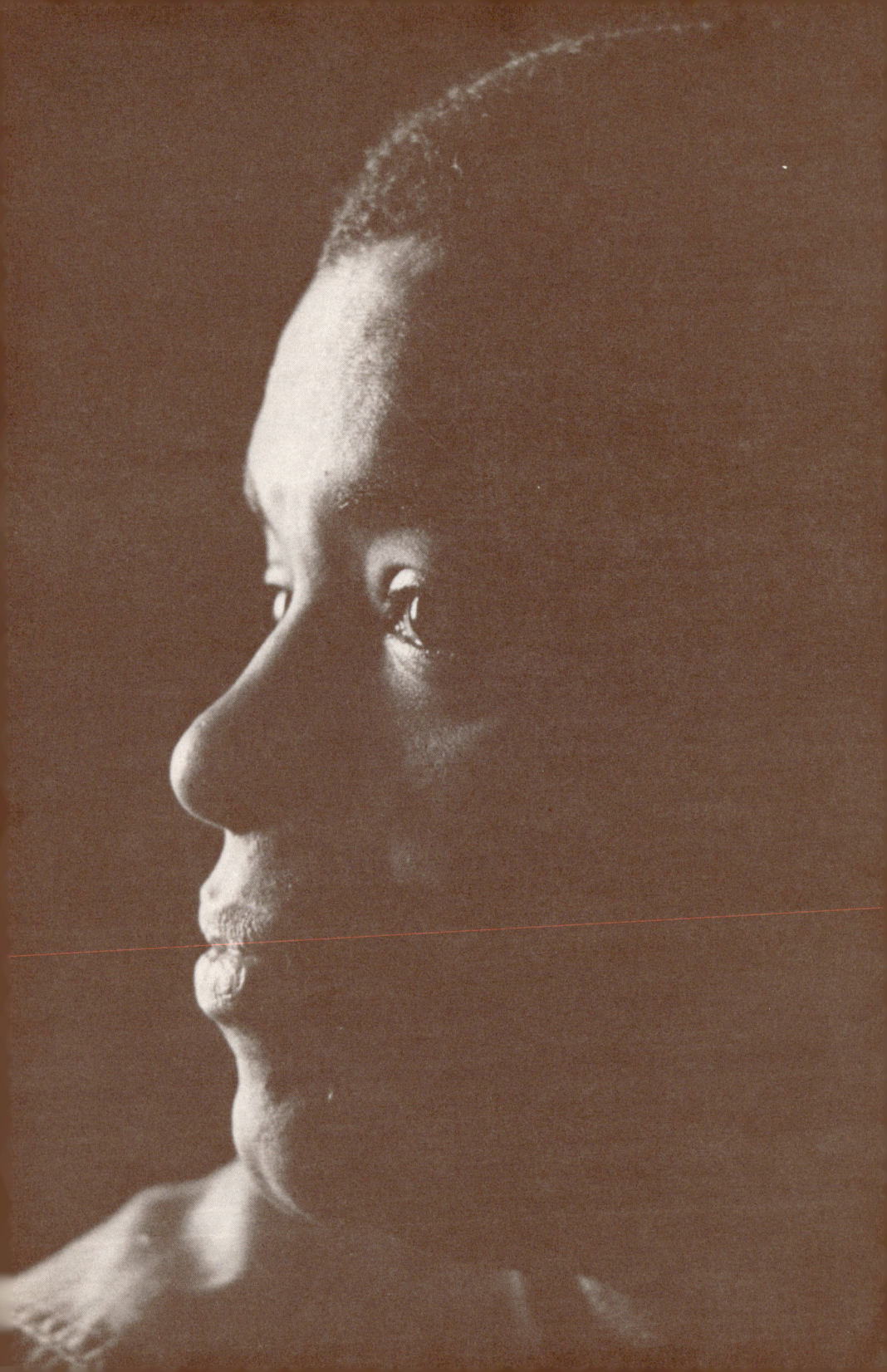

just glad I have someone to ask; so many kids today don't seem to have anyone.

Being a teenager is almost like being in a constant state of questioning. I feel so caught between being young and being grown up, between wanting to be free to make my own decisions and lead my own life and wanting to be sheltered from making any decisions. Most of my questions are the result of being caught in the middle. Why is it, I wonder, that people my age, who have to spend so much time and energy just getting used to their changing bodies, should have all these other things to worry about at the same time? Questions like, "Is the way I feel about the opposite sex normal?" or, "Am I normal?" often spin through my head, God. I feel so awkward at times that I think other kids can't possibly feel like I do. Do others ask, "What will I be after I finish high school?" or, "Will there be another war just when I'm ready to take on an adult role?" I even wonder, God, if it's normal to ask so many questions! Sometimes I wonder if I'm normal mentally; I worry so much when I get depressed, and sometimes I wonder if I'm completely sane, God. I could sure use some answers for a change.

Or religious questions. "Is my church the 'right' church?" "Is Jesus really my Savior?" "Is there really a heaven, and will I go there?" These questions fill me with hope and fear at the same time. And questions about love and death and fear and . . . well, You know what I'm thinking, God.

I'm coming on pretty heavy, God. I'm sorry, but I need You to straighten me out. Oh, I know You won't drop answers down in a balloon or answer me all at once, but You have a way of saying, "I'm here; I'm in control. You are My child and I'm not about to let you be overwhelmed." Wow, God, keep reminding me of that;

fill me with faith and confidence. Remind me that You are with me and that even if my questions won't go away, You won't either. That's all I need. Thanks, God.

Religion

Most of my life I've been connected with the church and with religion in some way. But I guess I never really gave it much thought, God. I know that sounds bad, but it was a habit; I didn't have to think.

I'm thinking more now, God, and I'm feeling different too. I need to talk to You about some of the thoughts and feelings I have. It really bothers me that there are so many churches—I don't mean numbers, but kinds of churches. Is only one the right one? Are several right? Or are they all wrong? I know that I've grown up believing that I was in the right one—sometimes I thought it was the only right one—but why would anyone knowingly go to a wrong church? That makes me wonder if mine is right!

And churches do a lot of things differently. They believe different things and worship in different ways. Is there a right way or time to baptize or take Communion? Or a right age? Are these the important things, or is what I believe important?

Even the music differs in churches, God. Hymns have different words and different melodies; they're played on different kinds of instruments. I guess I always thought at least the music would be the same, God. Does one kind please You more than other kinds? And while some churches are formal and quiet, others are loud and informal. Which do You prefer, God? Or does it make any difference?

I know the Bible is the key, but it sure doesn't explain all these things. Are they important? I know the Bible says Jesus died for my sins and that I'll be saved if I believe that. That's going to mean a lot more than just people in my church are going to be saved. Doesn't that mean we ought to try harder to get along with other believers here on earth too? And with unbelievers? I sometimes get pretty tired of all the arguing over what seems to be pretty unimportant. But how do I know if it's unimportant to You, God?

Maybe that's why Bible study is so important. Maybe it can really help me see what You say in Your Word. I know people read things in different ways, but at least we'd be looking in the right place for answers and not relying so much on our own judgment. Guide me, God, as I search Your Scriptures. Give me wisdom and give me faith; cause me always to hold tightly to the truth of what Jesus did for me. That can never change, God, regardless of what different churches say and do.

Sex

It's almost as hard, God, to talk to You about sex as it is to talk to my folks. But since You gave us our bodies and our feelings and the means of reproduction, You must be the Expert in the area. Sex scares me, God, and yet I'm so curious, so filled with mixed feelings. I want to be normal and have others see me as normal, but wow, what conflicts fill me. I know sex can be used in right and wrong ways—like most all of Your gifts—but society somehow has made sex different from all other things.

I know I'm growing up. I see the changes in my body.

I feel feelings I haven't felt before. I hear others talking and pretend I'm not interested, but I am. You bet I am. And some of what I hear and a lot of what I see scares me. Am I ready for something like this? Will I be attractive to others? Will I always bring dignity to myself, to others? Can I govern my own desires by my respect for the feelings and wishes of others? Can I say no even when I think yes? God, I am sometimes so confused by what I know about waiting for marriage and by what I'd like to try right now. I know it's right and probably best to wait, but it's so easy to ask why when so many others don't.

Help me, God! I want to keep my body pure and chaste in matters of sex. I do want it to be Your temple. But I don't want to be "out of it" either. Give me the strength to stand firm in my principles. Give me the courage to say no when I know certain actions are wrong. Help me discuss sex with my parents and others who care about me in a way that won't embarrass either them or me. Help me talk about sex with people my age that I respect, even with those that I date and may face temptations with. And since I am a sinful human being, and since my thoughts and actions are sometimes sinful, forgive me, God. And help me ask forgiveness of those I offend. Help me live a life that pleases You and pleases my own conscience. Remind me that Jesus lived on earth too, and let me remember that He never gave in to sin, even though He was tempted. Let me make Him my model, and let Him give me wisdom to know what to do and strength to do it in a way that pleases You. Thanks for listening, God, and thanks for helping.

Tensions

It really gets to me when an adult says something like, "Boy, I wish I were your age again, no problems, no worries." If only they knew. You know I have a lot of problems, God, and You know how they often tie me in knots. I need these times with You to loosen a few.

I know I can bring all my troubles to You, and I know You'll help. You do all the time. But even that doesn't make them stop coming. One day it's classes; the next it's my friends. Then it's money or a job, and then it's a quarrel with my family. I try—I really do try—to avoid these things, or pray, or think positively, but it's just not that easy. I worry a lot about my health, my sanity, and even whether it's worth going on.

Adults can't believe that kids think about suicide. They can't imagine that we actually would do something like that. Don't they read newspapers, God? Do they really believe that only someone else's kid would think about or actually commit suicide? I'm glad You know better, God. And when I have these thoughts, it helps me to know that You are taking them seriously. But it also scares me that I do think about driving into a bridge, or taking an overdose of something, or using a gun when things seem to have fallen apart. Why am I so frightened of life, God? Why do my insides get tied in knots so often? I know I'm not the only one, and that scares me even more. Can You help me understand and overcome this?

Maybe that's why You spend so much time listening

and watching out for teenagers. You must know that we're the vulnerable ones, the ones who feel robbed of childhood security before we're really ready for adult responsibility. Society puts so many pressures on us—to look right or smell right, to speak and write correctly, to get a job of some kind, to think of college, to not goof up. Adults so often throw up their hands in despair at our temper, our moodiness, our insults, our ups and downs. They don't understand that all of this is our reaction to the tensions. But You understand. You don't throw up Your hands; You see and hear me all the time, even when I forget all about You or doubt that You exist.

But You're near, always. I feel You when I lock my door and sit alone in my room, when I cry into my pillow, when I drive up and down the streets thinking, or when I find a tree to sit under way out in the middle of nowhere. And I hear You at those times saying words of comfort to me. I feel Your arm around me, Your hand holding mine. I might not admit it to anyone else that I need my hand held, but Yours feels awfully good right now. Thanks, God, I needed that!

Unbelief

If most of the people I know knew that I spent time talking to You like this, God, they'd think that I'd lost my senses. If they knew that I trust in You to guide me through these years, they'd say things like, "When are you going to grow up?" That's what so many feel about You, God, like something you put away when you grow up. They don't believe You even exist, and they certainly don't believe You have the power to control all things in the world.

I've tried to talk to them, to tell them about the prayers You've answered, the peace You bring, and the promise of heaven that You give because of Jesus. But when I say these things, they usually just laugh or scoff or say, "Well, if God is so strong and so loving, why do we have wars, or pain, or sin?" If I try to tell them that these things come from Satan and our own sins, not You, they just chuckle and look smug. After all, they don't believe in Satan either—or heaven or hell. I guess I get tired of even trying, and even worse, I sometimes wonder for a moment or two if they might not be right. I mean, what if You aren't real, what if death is the end, what if heaven and hell are just fantasy? Then I could live and do whatever I wanted. After all, I have only Your Word for evidence of Your existence—and the world itself, and me, and love, and beauty. Would they exist if You didn't? I know they wouldn't!

Maybe doubts like that aren't all bad. I think they give me a chance to imagine a world and a life without You. And when I think about living that way, that would be hell already. My doubts help assure me that You are very real, that You do love me and all people, that You are in control, that You did send Jesus to die for me and to rise again, and that You really did prepare a place in heaven for me and will take me there when I die.

I know I won't be able to convince everyone of what I know, but maybe one person will see my life and hear my words. Even one person is more than enough reason to keep on sharing with others what I believe. Don't let me ever get discouraged and quit, God! Give me the words that will get them to listen, and move them to accept You. Use me, God, as You wish. Make me a more effective voice for You.

Vulgarity

God, I decided to just listen today to the language people around me are using. You wouldn't believe the vulgarity and profanity that I heard! Well, I guess You'd believe it since I'm sure You heard it too. People my age, boys and girls alike, seem to delight in using words and phrases that I'd think would offend anyone. And I'm not excusing myself, God; I caught myself doing the same thing. It's like sex and the human body and Your name are just excuses to show off a warped vocabulary. What's wrong with us, God? What can I do to stop using such language and to help get others to think a bit before they talk that way? I'm not trying to sound like a prude or a "holy-holy"; it's just the first time I really listened and thought about what I was hearing. I'm ashamed, God.

What is the reason? I don't think it was always like this, not so out in the open, at least. Is it television? Or books? Is it the moral decay of the nation? Is it adult language that we are trying to copy so that we can at least sound like adults? Or is it mostly us and our attitude toward ourselves and others? Maybe it's just a sign that we aren't really happy with ourselves or with our lives. Whatever it is, when I think about it, I'm disgusted with myself and with my friends and other teenagers. And You, God, must be sad and angry at the same time. I know You don't approve. Can You show me a way to stop my own foulness and help others who down deep may feel the same way?

I know the words aren't new; they're just a lot more out in the open. There was a time when dirty language was supposed to make boys seem like men, but now the girls use it as much as boys. It's like we all find a warped pleasure in shocking others by our knowledge and our daring. Will You help? Please?

I have Your Word, and I know Your will. But many times I don't even notice when I swear. Help me at least notice it when I do. That would be a start. Then remind me before I say something, and stop me before I do it. And help me finally get to the point where I won't even notice that I *don't* swear. Work in me and through me, God. Let my light shine; let others notice that I don't use bad language any more, and let them learn from me. When I slip, forgive me, and let me encourage others who control their tongues. Keep me from making fun of those who do not curse and swear. I know this is one more sin that Jesus died for, God; help me overcome it. I know with Your help, I can.

Wisdom

I just remembered a Bible story, God, about Solomon, just after he became king of Israel. He prayed to You for wisdom—not wealth or happiness or power. Just wisdom. And I remember that You were very pleased with his prayer; You even gave him all the other things too. I'd like You to give me wisdom too, not like Solomon, but just enough to help me make the decisions that face me and will continue to face me every day.

It's easy to confuse knowledge and wisdom. I've been in school for a lot of years, and I'm learning a lot of

things, a lot of facts, a lot of skills, a lot of ideas. But this is only knowledge. I need wisdom, the ability to use my knowledge wisely. Can You help me remember the difference?

For example, I know that smoking is harmful to my health; it even says that on the package. I know it's wrong to drive more than 55 miles per hour; signs along every road constantly remind me. This is knowledge, and I need to know such facts. But I and a lot of others still might smoke or drive too fast. Knowledge hasn't helped at all. That's why I need wisdom, God. I need to consider these facts and make a *wise* decision; I need to take everything into consideration and decide on the basis of what is good for me and pleasing to You. Some people might call wisdom "common sense," although I don't think it's too common these days.

Wisdom involves judgment, God. I think that sometimes knowledge can even hamper judgment, get in the way of wisdom. And are there times, God, when facts or laws say I should *not* do something and wisdom says I ought to do so anyway? Like when I feel I must defend someone who is legally wrong but is being unjustly treated? I think so, God, but I can't make these hard decisions without You, without the wisdom that only You can give.

And finally, God, Your wisdom can overcome the knowledge of the world that would deny Your power, even deny that You exist. Give me the courage to be "wise unto salvation," even when the knowledge of the world laughs at You and me and gives all kinds of "evidence" of Your nonexistence.

Guide me always, God, and give me just enough wisdom to distinguish between Your ways and the ways of the world, and let me be a model of faith and courage for others.

(X) Pornography

This is a tough one, God. It's not just a tough letter to find a word for, but it's a tough subject that I've decided to talk about with You. But I do think that even if I'm stretching things a bit, it is a fair use of this letter. I see a lot of signs these days saying "X-rated" this or "triple-X-rated" that. It's real, God, and my pretending pornography doesn't exist won't make it go away. And let's face it, a 17 or 18 age limit doesn't amount to very much. I can get books or magazines or movies of this kind without anyone ever asking about my age.

It seems so easy to know what to do about pornography. I know it's wrong, sinful, and inappropriate for a Christian of any age. But it's there, God, and it's real, and it offers a temptation of the toughest kind for someone my age.

I know it's not wrong for me to be interested in sex, to wonder what it is like; and I'd be lying if I said sex and nudity and things like that aren't interesting to me. After all, sex is Your gift to us, and You made us different—men and women. It offers pleasure in addition to providing the means of reproduction. And I know that it's awfully hard *not* to look at pictures or books or films that show or talk about sex. I really need to feel You near me at those times, God; I need Your firm nudge in the other direction when these things are available. And I need instruction in the kind of attitude toward sex that pleases You.

You gave Your gift of sex to use properly, and You

set the proper limits for it within marriage. You created it for a giving, not taking kind of love. So much of what pornography offers is not love but lust, not giving at all, but the worst kind of taking and using of another person. What You created beautiful, people have made ugly and dirty. What You created as a special gift, we have turned into sin.

God, help me to recognize pornography for what it is, a sinful trap that distorts sex and misleads those who come into contact with it. Give me the strength to pass by the deceiving titles, pictures, and advertisements and turn instead to the picture of love and sex that You desire. Help me wait until the time is right, and bring me then a loving relationship that pleases You, my spouse, and me. Thank You, God, for Your help.

Youth

Maybe it's unnecessary to talk to You about youth; almost all these conversations with You have been on that subject. But yet, God, we are special people, unlike children and unlike adults. Sometimes we act like both, and sometimes we are neither. I don't understand myself and other teenagers much of the time; only someone like You can, and I ask Your help. Please listen.

Something must happen to our whole personality about this age. I feel so elated one moment, so depressed the next. I feel like shouting for joy, and then I feel like crying. I feel agile and athletic half the time and like a complete uncoordinated clod the other half. For every moment I feel grown up, I have at least one in which I feel like an ignorant baby. Just when I feel confident about something—school, the way I look, some talent I have—I do something that destroys all that confidence in one short moment. No wonder teachers and parents say teenagers are the hardest people in the world to get along with, the most difficult to teach. And no wonder I'm grateful that You take the time to listen to me and ease my concerns.

Why is it, God, that just when I have the most new experiences to contend with that I feel least courageous? Why am I so tongue-tied when I want to speak my best, so clumsy when I want to impress others with my grace?

I really do have good intentions, but I goof up so often that others must think I spend extra time each day just inventing problems for them. I know I lash out at those who try to give me gentle suggestions on how to eat, how to dress, how to walk, but I feel so defensive, so certain that everyone is deliberately picking on me to help make me miserable. And, God, I think that most young people feel like I do.

Thank goodness I have You, God! You actually can understand me, even when no one else does. Although I have troubles, You see that I don't have any more than I can handle. If You think I'm hanging on to You for dear life, You're right. If I let go for even a moment, I'll trip over something and fall flat on my face. Give me strength, God, to make it through these years. Build my courage and my confidence. The years ahead look awfully dark at times, but if You're with me, I'll somehow make it. Please don't get tired of picking me up. Even if others lose patience with me—and who can really blame them—I know You're not yet finished making me what I am going to be. And that's encouraging, God!

(Z) Death

Excuse me, God, for cheating a bit on "Z," but I'm not concerned about "zebras" or "zoos" anymore. It is the last letter, God, and death is the last thing that will happen to me in this life. And death is what I'm thinking about right now.

Older people don't realize that I think about death. But they're wrong. I think about it a lot; all kids do. Sometimes we try to act "cool" about it or joke about it, but we think about it often. You see, God, we notice death. We see our grandparents die, maybe even someone closer; and if they're older, maybe we ignore it or pretend to. But I've had friends die—or friends of friends; kids my age do die. Sometimes—often—it's a car wreck; sometimes sickness. But death isn't reserved for old people, even when I like to pretend it is. I know it's real for me too. I don't expect it to happen to me, but it could. Anytime. And when I realize that, I think about it and how it could cut off just like that all my plans, all my dreams about growing up.

Sometimes knowing I will die sooner or later makes me wonder why I should even go on living. Why should I study or work or get married if it's all going to end? Why not just quit now? It sure would save a lot of pain and disappointment and trouble. And then at other times I find myself asking how You can dare let young people die without their having a real chance to live.

I'm sorry, God. I shouldn't think like that. But death boggles my mind. I try to imagine what death is like, but

I can't—no one can. But about the time I get really bothered by it, I remember you talking about "working while it's day" or "being faithful to death," and I know there's a reason, even if it's not clear, for me to use the time I have.

Help me accept death, God, both my own and others. But don't let that acceptance of its reality bother me so much that I can't do anything. Help me live—today, tomorrow, as long as I have. Help me find and fulfill the purpose You have for me. Let me enjoy all the beauties and pleasures that You have created for my joy. Help me through the pain and trouble that exist because sin exists. That's what You want me to do, I know. Let me see death as the end of this life, but let me also see it as the beginning of a better life. Help me live this day as though it will be my last day—I know it might be; but let me also live it as though I will live forever, for because of the death and resurrection of Jesus, I know I will. Amen, God, and thanks for listening.